KIDS OWN NatureBook

Baby Wild Animals

Heritage House Publishing Company Ltd.
#108 - 17665 66A Avenue
Surrey, BC V3S 2A7
www.heritagehouse.ca

Heritage House Publishing Company Ltd.
PO Box 468
Custer, WA
98240-0468

LIBRARY AND ARCHIVES CANADA CATALOGUING IN PUBLICATION

Schmidt, Dennis, 1921–
Baby wild animals / photographs by Dennis and Esther Schmidt.

ISBN 978-1-894974-66-0

1. Animals—Infancy—Juvenile literature.
I. Schmidt, Esther, 1922– II. Title.

QL49.S36 2009   j591.39   C2008-908132-3

LIBRARY OF CONGRESS CONTROL NUMBER: 2009920321

Printed in Canada

Heritage House acknowledges the financial support for its publishing program from the Government of Canada through the Book Publishing Industry Development Program (BPIDP), Canada Council for the Arts and the province of British Columbia through the British Columbia Arts Council and the Book Publishing Tax Credit.

Baby Wild Animals

Photographs by Dennis and Esther Schmidt

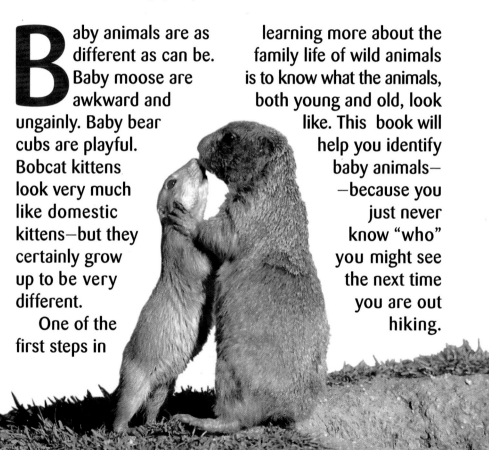

Baby animals are as different as can be. Baby moose are awkward and ungainly. Baby bear cubs are playful. Bobcat kittens look very much like domestic kittens—but they certainly grow up to be very different.

One of the first steps in learning more about the family life of wild animals is to know what the animals, both young and old, look like. This book will help you identify baby animals——because you just never know "who" you might see the next time you are out hiking.

Chipping Sparrow

Whitetailed Fawn

Cougar Kitten

Baby Ground Squirrels

Swan Cygnets

Merlin Chicks

Coyote Pup

Bighorn Lambs

Red Fox Kits

Black Bear Cubs

Bobcat Kittens

Loggerhead Shrike Nestlings

Elk Calf

Bighorn Lamb

Bighorn Lambs

Mule Deer Fawn

Mule Deer Fawn

Mountain Goat Kid

Black Bear Cubs

Canada Goose Gosling

Wolf Pups

**Baby
Woodpeckers**

Baby Hummingbirds

Moose Calf

Prairie Dog Pup

Baby Rabbit

Pronghorn Antelope Fawn

Osprey Chicks

Saw Whet Owlet

Avocet Chicks

Elk Calf

Cedar Waxwing Nestlings

Baby Northern Flickers

Cougar Kitten